WE ARE THE UNDERGROUND
Michael Anthony Adams, Jr.

SIX SEEDS PRESS
Baltimore, MD

First Six Seeds Press Edition
Copyright © 2018 Michael Anthony Adams, Jr.

Originally Published as *We Are the Underground* by Israfel Sivad by CreateSpace Independent Publishing Platform
November 2018

Current Edition Published by Six Seeds Press,
Baltimore, MD
February 2022

"Epiphany" and "We Are the Underground" originally appeared in the Spring/Summer 2017 issue of *The Stray Branch*. "Eleven Variations on a Theme" originally appeared in the Winter 2017 edition of *Badlands Literary Journal*. "A Straight Line Runs Through It All" originally appeared on www.ExaminingTheOdd.com on 4/23/2018.

All rights reserved.

ISBN: 978-1-952240-15-7

Cover Design © 2018 PJ Adams
Portrait of Michael Anthony Adams, Jr. © 2014 PJ Adams

Also by Michael Anthony Adams, Jr. and Published by Six Seeds Press

Fiction:
The Adversary's Good News: A Novel
Psychedelicizations: Short Stories
The American Apocalypse: Short Stories
Crossroads Blues: A Novel
The Cars Behind, Beside Us: Short Stories
Welcome to the Modern World, Charlie: Short Stories
Notes from the Idle Mind: Short Stories

Nonfiction:
Disorder: An Avant-Garde Memoir of Psychosis, Healing and Love

Poetry:
We Are the Underground: Poems
From Now to You: Haiku
Recipe for a Future Theogony: Poems
Indigo Glow: Poems
The Tree Outside My Window: Poems
At the Side of the Road: Poems
Soundtrack for the New Millennium: A Poem

www.6SeedsPress.com

MICHAEL ANTHONY ADAMS, JR.

We Are the Underground
For Louise
... who taught me the Nature of Spirit

We Are the Underground

Contents

I. Inspired Poems, Part 1
1. *Petra* — 13
2. How I Long for My Youth… — 15
3. INRI — 17
4. Torture — 19
5. The House Around the Corner — 20
6. Sketch for a Future Poet — 22
7. Clarion Call — 24
8. Epiphany — 26

II. The "Zodiac" Cycle, Sunrise
1. 888 — 31
2. Taking Pleasure in the Mind — 32
3. Doves Sat on the Egg Until It Hatched — 34
4. The Orgasmatron — 36
5. The Jungle — 38
6. Or Were You Always Me? — 39
7. The Fourth Labor — 41
8. Somewhere Between Life and Death — 43
9. Praying for Saturn's Return — 44
10. The Wild Wilderness of Oz — 45
11. Following the Eldest Root — 47
12. Between Humans and Beasts — 49

III. Alignment
1. Emerald City — 53
2. Caesar and Christ — 54
3. We Are the Underground — 55
4. I Am the Future — 57

    5. Upon This Star   58

IV. The "Zodiac" Cycle, Sunset
    1. Room 101   61
    2. At War with Tamerlane   62
    3. Fearful Synteny   64
    4. The Ninth Prophecy   66
    5. Excalibur   67
    6. Bathsheba, Part I   68
    7. Upon First Transliterating the Theoretical Form   70
    8. A Straight Line Runs Through It All   71
    9. Eleven Variations on a Theme   72
    10. Hesperides   74
    11. After the "Brainfreeze"   75
    12. Zen   76

V. Inspired Poems, Part 2
    9. Of Dragons and Unicorns   79
    10. Shesha   81
    11. Athena's Coming Full-Term   82
    12. Under the Bodhi Tree   84
    13. Our Holy Plane   87
    14. A History   90
    15. A Response to Tyranny   91
    16. The Morning's Light   93

We Are the Underground

I.
Inspired Poems, Part 1

Petra

This river flows through
the middle of my soul,
though I barely pay it any mind.

This cityscape exists
at my edges of consciousness,
unconsciously governing my thoughts.

My actions are not my own.
They run through You to
deeper pastures and bayous.
From the Pacific Ocean, I
flowed to merge my stream
with Yours. Up the great
Mississippi, I came, the same
path my genes wound to run
away from you, looking for work.
We never found it; now we've returned.

I will spin my paddlewheel yet
again. I will churn the locomotive
yet again. I will follow the worn
paths of my ancestors to the heart
of this mystery where I will rebuild
the skyscrapers that broke the
tongues of my fallen kin. There
is nothing that will give me the
release I seek. There is nothing
that will fulfill my deep-seated fantasies.

This ramshackle Virginia

shack gave birth to my history,
yet I will never share its bond.

My destiny resides on the other
side of this promised land, where
Moses set his weary feet down to rest.

How I Long for My Youth…

How I long for my youth…
When knowledge unwound at the tips of my fingers,
and dreams united the kingdoms of the world.
How I long for my youth.

How I long for my youth!
Where I could place my eye inside your mind
so you could see the colors as I saw them then –
toys of cloud rocketships puffy against the Blue Lord's
  backdrop.
How I long for my youth,
and for the thrill of those outlaw, naked ages
that never could be seen by the bearded intruders
from beyond the veil of the canopy of a daylit starlight
  night.

For it was in my youth
when I cracked open the egg of my mind's shell
and discarded its contents like a yolk's bloody embryo
to further feed my youth.

To say youth's hour is done is the furthest thing from the
  truth.
Our ears still bleed to be told we can't swim in the nude…
Our Fathers still won't take a look at what we do.
No. I do not long for my youth!
When shall I recite the poem of the cave's golden
  paintings?
When shall I find time to paint the music of the spheres?
When shall I discover the lotus hidden inside the stone?
No! I do not long for my youth.

No… I do not long for my youth.
For dreams are still the substance the world is made of,
and knowledge is hidden in the particles of those truths.
No. I do not long for my youth…

INRI

The child does not realize he is a burden
with the weight of the world upon his shoulders.
The child does not realize he is a burden
that his mother forever carries in her womb.

The child does not realize he is the hero
who humanity has waited to beat and kill.
The child does not realize he is the hero
whose brothers will make him as impotent as they.

[While I watched the little boy cross the street, alone, so
    unhappy with his too long-ago-lost friend,
I heard the fears buried beneath his mother's tone reveal
    that someday, indeed, this also would end.]

The child does not realize he is his father.
For, the child remains a father to the elder.
The child does not realize he is his father,
and the lies of his father shall be omitted…

The child does not realize he is yet a ghost,
but still, he asks his friend to play along with him.
The child does not realize he is yet a ghost
that the entire world will soon learn how to see.

The child does not realize he is himself still
a boy who will never grow to be an adult.
The child does not realize he is himself still.
Everything else exists as a mere fantasy.

The child does not realize he is the savior

for himself because, in truth, there is no one else.
The child does not realize he is the savior
of a world that's never asked for salvation.

The child's only aware he is the butterfly
itself, verily, flitting in front of his nose.
The child's only aware he is the butterfly
he watched hatch from the pupa in his own backyard.

Torture

Torture me.
Torture me slowly again…
Take my soul from my body.
Through pain – you could make the pain stop.
And then, start the pain again… again, I need your torture.

Cut my tongue from me, pierce my flesh, draw and quarter
    me.

I believe your torture will make me more truly me…
More truly free from the crimes I've committed:
Crimes of politics, romance, flesh, blood.
Then, I could love
this world.

The House Around the Corner

Around the corner, everything was inverted:
The living room was where the kitchen should be.
The piano was in the fireplace, but still
I threw my ball against the outside wall.

Because you were nowhere to be found.

I went looking for you in the cupboards…
only to find the rats who subsequently
became my best friends there, scuttling
through these childish palms – my Sunday trees
had grown into stumps whose woods would
never blossom again. You broke my heart, then.

And today, I want its scattered shards to mend.

We're drawing dreams from every corner of this world,
to paint a portrait I believe you could make real:
The crucifixion of the boy with butterfly wings,
interred, protected by your exoskeleton…
For, the portrait itself is you: my Holy Spirit,
which will always know there is no end to this show.

Why would you expect anything different?

The real world is the ideal. The ideal world
is the real. When Gautama touched his gnarled toe
to the ground, he revealed this jeweled universe
I live in, alone, with you. In the beginning,
there were two, red and black, servants
in time, nameless angels both of them: a rhyme?

No. It's subtler than that… subtler, even, than that.

Jack Kerouac, John Donne, T.S. Eliot –
Modernity's martyrs like Charles Baudelaire
or James Joyce or you, hypocrite reader,
my semblance, my brother… I did it all
only for you. So that you wouldn't have to
go through everything you're going through.

But I am not the king of this seventh heaven.

I am merely their Adversary, Thrice-Majestic
Satan, the man, the serpent, Adam –
simultaneous Alpha and Omega;
simultaneous generator and destroyer.

The devil lived in the house around the corner.

Sketch for a Future Poet

This poem is a sketch of me
trying to liberate myself again.

To write as if I'd never heard language before…
To love as if I'd never seen a body before…
To live as if I'd never experienced this world before.

I believe…

Someday, nobody will believe
that, once upon a time, somebody
could have been so vibrant and alive.

Someday, nobody's eyes will gaze
upon the dark scratches that
sketched out these words you read.

Someday, nobody will know,
any longer, the veins on the hand
who wrote this poem.

Someday, nobody will caress,
any longer, the fingers that
held a pen to write these lines.

Someday, nobody's face will
be cupped by this palm
completed by these words it untangled.

Someday, nobody will believe
that, once upon a time, somebody
could have been so vibrant and alive.

Do you believe?

Will you live as if you'd never experienced love before?
Will you love as if you'd never seen a body before?
Will you write as if you'd never heard language before?

This poem is a sketch of you
trying to liberate yourself again.

Clarion Call

My lips are 15,000 years old;
my tongue is made of tempered steel.
I am the Angel of the Apocalypse
sent to force the devil himself to kneel.

I am the Angel of the Apocalypse,
the star that burns as bright as mourning.
I am the sun setting with evening's tide;
the light that keeps the dark from forming.

I am the sun setting with evening's tide,
a reflection cast by the full moon's glow.
I am the shadow always at your left-hand side,
the dream you sleep but never know.

I am the shadow always at your left-hand side,
a reflection cast by the full moon's glow.
I am the sun setting with evening's tide,
the star that burns as bright as mourning.
I am the Angel of the Apocalypse;
my tongue is made of tempered steel…

And I have come here for *You*.

My lips are 15,000 years old.
Sent to force the devil himself to kneel,
I am the Angel of the Apocalypse,
the light that keeps the dark from forming.
I am the sun setting with evening's tide:
the dream you sleep but never know.

The dream you sleep but never know

are the holes I bore in the eyes of God,
a reflection cast by the full moon's glow,
the meridian sun burning noon day's heat…

The light that keeps the dark from forming
is the source that glows inside my soul,
the star that burns as bright as mourning –
Lucifer: knowledge in its unbounded form

sent to force the devil himself to kneel.
I was forged in the flames of the dawn of time;
my tongue is made of tempered steel,
and midnight's temple is *Set* to rise.

Epiphany

She keeps telling me my words
as if they were her own,
which they are.

Because she's invigorated me.

She pulls poetry from my body
as if it were love itself,
which it is.

Because she's liberated me.

Let me let you into our world…
Where dragons rule the break of dawn
and robots cradle our minds in sleep.
In between — a whole universe exists.
Algae grows across our lungs…
Plants fulfill our bloodstreams.
Our hair is made of dandelion sprouts:
And all the animals roam free.

Your liberation is my dream…
Reptilian — stoic as a plank…
You awaken, downwards like a dog
to curl up as a child in pose.
Your dream is my liberation…
From the tyranny of myself…
From the apocalypse I inhabit
filled with childhood fears.

Kundalini unraveled, intertwined us both
in a providential web we created

where the beacon burned atop a hill,
leading me to you. Together, we left…
Ran away down 95 South,
got lost in New York City,
but we'll cross the ocean together,
traverse this entire undiscovered country.

You string poetry through me
like the end and beginning,
which you are.

Because you've invigorated me.

You create the words on my tongue
like a muse
named Epiphany.

Because you've liberated me.

II.
The "Zodiac" Cycle, Sunrise

888

You are Enki's child
who carved the Sun Stone
with a goat's horn…

A mysterious warrior
bearing the people's sorrow
amid Lord Shiva's embrace.

On this third month's
third day, you strangled
the serpent creating our universe.

Your mind is a pyramid.
Your tale's the ocean. Infinity
rests between your steps,

nestles into your many sets.
My positive approaches your negative
and adds up to the counter-intuitive.

You are the celestial ox
watering the earth:
a pure woman of emptiness.

The warring states are crying
upon your ramparts —
a trinity for nonbelievers.

While you sail across the heavens,
attack, withdraw, and reserve
yourself until my birth.

Taking Pleasure in the Mind

Father, lover, friend…
you've aged in your youth.
We left our home together last night
and traveled through history.
Drive on through the darkness
to lead me to your source…

Where the Ganges flows into the Nile…
Where you drop your cup and pour a winter's deluge
to drown the anointed, like Pharaoh's army,
in the middle… Where, stolen from the morning
sun, Helen attempts your rival. Sacrifice
your blood like wine tonight.

Let the forest shiver through your feathers, a vast
army of emptiness burning among
your lucky stars; this supernova explodes
inside my heart – firstborn to possess
the signs of life. Only the King Himself could
cast His gaze upon the yellow tip of our flame.

My cousin and I shall join your romance, though less
beneficent than you to us. *You* taught us
to not believe the priests, to trust ourselves
instead – the genius, the insane: completely
human with needs greater than your own. Independent,
emotionless to those of forgotten faith.

Yours is the Father of all
the gods: a fixed quality, an airy
element, a masculine nature adorned
in Saint Michael's robe. Your metal turns nuclear,

drowns me like lead, the primrose carnation
tattooed through your ankle into your blood,

which is mine. For, your body is
mine. Your mind sparks my own. We shared
each other last night until your light
burst through this darkness, incinerating
the world's newest age with the breath of
this dragon bleeding at your feet.

Doves Sat on the Egg Until It Hatched

The cup-bearer is seated at my right…
A horned beast reaches out to my left…
This oxygen is such an uncomfortable thing.

A circular saw passes through my torso…
I'm alone on the horizon's edge…
And I much prefer the salted sea.

It's the twelfth month
of the year, and this
is only the beginning.
This current age:
30° to absolute zero,
we'll start to boil.

Ptolemy's 39th horn
pierces my groin, but
there's nothing special
about me. I'm strangling
myself with the rope
leading to my own well.

In opposite directions,
I express your duality
as Typhon and Christ.
Aphrodite banished me
from Heaven; though,
I am her own son.

Atop your waiting sarcophagus, I recline…
My original doctrine was corrupted…
By poets, by priests and archaeologists.

You carved my name in Ephesus…
For, I protected your Platonic Forms…
The rock upon which this world is built.

My own mother sits
across the table from me,
and my companions
followed us in here.
We are the source of
everything you believe.

Jupiter is my father…
Neptune, my uncle.
I walked upon the moon
until you poisoned me
with your quicksilver
because I exalted love.

My brother's forked tail
will sting you. My sister,
she devours you. Together,
we're shape shifters,
adept at both the astral
and psychic planes.

In the sign of the Southern Cross…
There are now six more of us…
In fact, even I've turned into two.

There is no scientific basis for me…
I'm perceptive, emotional, yet reasonable…
The unfortunate one, drowning on land.

The Orgasmatron

You are the first... visible
until the end of time: a
new beginning for the
Fool's anniversary. Six
hours later every year,
you sound the trumpets
of War – the origin of life
itself. You are the cardinal
fire, scapegoat, perpetual
enemy of Venus. Exalting
the sun, you fell from
the house of the gods.

With your fleece of gold,
you water the earth: twin
inspector for oceanic life.
Galaxies interact within you.
Meteors shower from your
reign, encompassing every-
thing around you. You are
the Pharaoh, first – fertility,
creativity... The storyteller I
met once upon a time. When
you indicated my rebirth, our
priests dedicated *this* to you.

Not to be confused
with the "southern" fly,
you've been seen every-
where. Looking behind your-
self, running – you are the
polygon of twelve segments

who saved the regent's children
by bucking Hell from your back –
You crouched, head downturned…
Unformed and void, you rule
my mind, and now is your time.
(I met you, once, as a child.)

The Jungle

More muscular and aggressive,
this is the time of our lives.
Our bones are thicker, our feet —
larger. Our necks won't keep us
from the front line any longer.

Our eyes are armored. Our manes
are black and mature. Your music
has grown flat; we're blind to the
birth of your Lord. Move to provoke
us again, you who slaughtered our children.

In Sumer, we reached maturity. Prehistoric
peoples merged themselves with us, turned
us to the steeds for 18 of your gods. We
despise your superior attitudes. Equanimity
lies in our souls, which is why we beg
your mother for forgiveness, offer
her first-born our most prized possessions.

Not even the serpent's poison could
destroy us. We are your kings after
death, alive inside their hearts and minds.
The sun itself shines from *our* music,
the wings of our third eyes, our tongues.

Once upon a time, we led you
through the desert to be abandoned.
But we are jealous gods, punishing
gods who will visit the sins of the
Fathers upon their sons in the jungle.

Or Were You Always Me?

When we were children,
you revealed yourself to me –
In the vacant lot next door,
between the dirt clods you
threw in my face, I saw your
fangs and horns beneath
a cherub's lonely gaze.
I believed in you then.
The way you overleaped
the snake to make it atop
our playground slide first.
The way you spit as you
spoke, and taught me to
eat plastic grapes. The way
the watermelon seed sprouted
that vine from out your stomach.
The way you survived maggots,
earthquakes, and World War III.

I believe in you today:
the caretaker for the garden,
my father's final resting place,
where he threw us into heaven
while we laughed and played.
It was so simple back then when
he broke my nose, and a tornado
carried me away to where the toads,
rats, and lizards roamed. Amid
sharks, we've found our freedom.
In waves, we were imprisoned by
the witch who marked us with

her nails, that blind witch who
set us free. There's no freedom
in our world today. I'm bound
to you bound to her bound to me,
united by blood and ancestry…
That witch must know the truth.

Is it that I was always you?
Or were you always me?

The Fourth Labor

With gills like feathers, we're
found in the brooks and streams
where fresh water runs, feeding
on the living and dead – animals
and plants of 115 million years.

Starving, consuming our own
exoskeletons, we're your food,
your bait, your pets. The bass
and bluegill… your fish are our
enemies; your mold is our plague.

We've read every letter of
your alphabet, traversing Alpha
to Omega. Beta is where our bee-
hive shone brightest: the cancer
already growing in your breast.

Eyeless, we see well enough
in the dark to infect your hero's
foot, to be immortalized for our
work with the serpent by your
God's own goddess in the south.

Sentimental about the past,
we're emotional, responding
to love; your sensations reach
our minds with such clarity, we
don't doubt them for an instant.

Ruled by the moon, our intuitive

powers are excellent: the source
of the waters in which we live.
Look for us at 90° tonight – our
death silently creeping into you.

Somewhere Between Life and Death

My claws will slice through your armor
to leave you sitting still in a psych ward,
smoking cigarettes while your children
run panicked through the wilderness.

My golden fur is impervious to your attacks…
I'll look serene and pristine as you vomit
your insecurities onto me in a court of law
when you take me for everything I'm worth.

My father was a typhoon who came of age
during war, smoking charcoal, delivering
heat in the wintertime with a wink and
a grin women half his age find seductive.

My mother was a nymph with glancing
eyes and a serpent's baby rattle who birthed
me in the mountains where I spent my youth
blindly echoing sermons among crags and cliffs.

I lie somewhere between life and death, a
question mark posed to you in the form of
a sickle when you met me in the graveyard
where I told you I lost my virginity at your age.

To every culture, I am the lion, violent star
of Bacchus, seated on my throne, feasting
on your flesh to celebrate the end of summer
where you and I ride wild in the hurricane winds.

Praying for Saturn's Return

Last to leave the earth
destroyed by your impiety,
I remain pure to this day.

First, father executed mother,
leaving me imprisoned in
a bronze reign to establish

the Church as *I* see fit…
poets and playwrights, children
for whom I bear nothing

but your culture's renaissance:
joy and love, oriented only
by my "non-mathematical"

revelation of your planet's
staid motion. Discover!
Track your Beast – analytic,

observant – through the night
perceptive with memories
to balance your physics.

The Wild Wilderness of Oz

These scales before my eyes
keep me blinded to the sun.
In a metallic, blackened justice
I dwell, weighing your heart
against this feather, my master, you're heavier.

On that grassy knoll, I fell
asleep – *The Book of Chuang Tzu*
open at my childish feet, Public Enemy
#1 clanging chords through my veins, criss-
crossing my wrists: Extermination Day.

The mantis preys upon me:
a sacrifice to the Goddess of Light.
It is my own desire to be
devoured, in prayer, like an eternal lover,
like this book I always wished
to discover open inside my soul.
Could you read it to me aloud, this time, again?

Like you always did throughout my childhood,
holding my open palm between your trembling fingers
in the backseat of my father's Buick,
like you did for all the other men?
Like when you saw the Lord gaze at you
from His lonely eyes hidden within that fallen tree…

The same Lord my grandfather met
when he decided to be reborn to *this* life.
In the reign of the Antichrist, on this hellish plane,
he waited only for me. For three times four

long years, he waited only for me.

In a hospital bed, to be sacrificed,
a halo around his balding head, in a robe
of white, upon the burning coals of this
downward slope – only to be born again,
here, with me, his nemesis, his twin.

Following the Eldest Root

You are my darkness
like a mystery sent to
curb humanity's pride.

In your heart, you are
the universe's only
celestial rival to War.

Discovered during primal
creation, you are Persia's
royal guardian to the West.

Your remains have been
found encased in amber
11 million years away.

Aside from your compatriots,
you predict the Fall as one
of Heaven's four guardians.

Your favor and disaster come
as you align your allies towards
the positive or the negative.

In the eighth division, you
battled on behalf of the sky
to protect us from evil.

Even though we've never
understood, I believe you
predict the world's course.

For, I am your claws
causing the earth to burn
as the sun's chariot dips.

Between Humans and Beasts

Born of the sun and rain,
they look like you, your brethren,
wild and lusty, uncultured
delinquents, overindulgent
drinkers prone to violence:
sired by a father consigned
to eternity upon a fiery wheel.

While you are…

A wise and gentle instructor
teaching heroic children the ancient arts
of your healing arrow forming the bridge
between humanity and beasts,

from out the East, your odyssey will
grow to be subsumed by the Strong,
the Great who return you to your
proper reign o'er the Western gods

where your precepts form the basis
of kindness and culture, devoid of
savage behavior while your powerful
weapons shed life's blood only to eat,

but as a sacrifice for the transgression
at civilization's core, this dart, licked by
the great serpent's poisoned nectar, shall
pierce your thigh to steal your eternal life.

While your brethren…

Remain a metaphor for conflict
between the lower and higher appetites
of all that is seen to precede every
shred of the culture I embrace and
cherish as the foundation of this
very world I create… looking to the
night sky to witness you beyond death.

III.
Alignment

Emerald City

This world has no room for poetry…
I whispered as I scuttled down the cracked
sidewalk between buildings blocking my view
of the world beyond my own greed and fear.

Crossing the street, I overleaped a puddle
beside the police cruiser flashing blue and red –
safety/dread – across the bricked up, boarded up facades
confounding connections with you whom I pass every day.

Inspiration drained out of my thoughts – inspired
by drab concrete, bustling bodies, and the subway
rumbling some place distant beneath my feet.
This world can't be the only one we imagine…

In a distant time and place, depending upon which
point is seen as the beginning, the Buddha
touched his toe to the ravaged earth, and all
the sages saw became a world of jeweled beauty.

I want to touch my pen to this blank page
and create the same, take all the hideousness
imprisoning us here and transform that glass
vessel broken by the street into an emerald city.

Caesar and Christ

I awoke with gospel singing through my breast today,
and I started contemplating the riddle called *"Caesar and Christ"*.
I felt the strains of a purple rain pattering upon my chest,
but the church next door remained silent and empty.
I stepped outside my building, sat down on my stoop,
and I lit one of the cigarettes I'm trying to give up.
My neighbors walked past me. I don't know any of their names,
but I silently nodded to them – *hello* – anyways.

I remembered – Last weekend, in the projects down the way,
police sirens cordoned off the streets. The bricks flashed red and blue:
wailing like the invaded citizens themselves were crying,
and I had no idea why any of this was happening.

Yesterday, a construction crew showed up at the park across the street.
They tore out the benches where my neighbors have sat since I moved in.
They didn't replace them with anything. They didn't put anything back.
Not even the internet could answer my questions after that.
I may be new to this city, but I'm not new to this place.
I lived somewhere before this, and I lived somewhere before that, too.
"This kid says some guy got stabbed in that alley last night,"
and I'm still wondering – Who's more important: Caesar or Christ?

We Are the Underground

Dear America,
I am your child,
and I am the underground.

… I hold the trumpet to my lips,
but I refuse to blow its silken
notes. All of the angels, they
all sing their songs through me:
I am the source of the abyss over
which the acrobats choose to leap.

The knowledge of live-evil spreads
grasping roots outside my window, runs
sap through my Father's French Horn, a
cool stream on which He played the song
just for me: a witch's bitchy brew just for me.
Childhood's tape deck still wears His odd
harmonics – hums even with His locomotive tune,

blows my shofar in the alcove of a fly's wing,
interred, protected by Your exoskeleton. Preying upon
spiders, You swore Your liquor was simple pomegranate
juice while We drove along chromatic XY avenues, ran
into bright Mississippi blues, never thinking of sin,
which is why I panicked the world would lock *You*
up in a different tomb like Beelzebub – to meet never again.

The foundation of my life weaves along the same
foundation as Yours, which is the answer
to which is perfect to purify Medusa as she reclines
across our bloody "forms", a trick Pythagoras

theorized with Heraclitus… Fluctuating at 90°,
serpents intertwined between the beats,
the sheets – You became me became

a two-headed beast, a mythology
of such a fantastic trinity that four
roots now reach through humanity's
soiled history to every continent upon
which Saint Paul safely danced while
Saint John imagined *Our* devolution…

Dear world,
We are your children,
and We are the underground.

I Am the Future

I am the future
of nature, this time, this place…
disappears like
moonlight at the break of day

to leave you
standing alone, clutching nothing
but air between
trembling fingers, no grass beneath

your toes; your eyes
breathe in the emptiness of this
vacuum I create
for you in this time, this place.

Upon This Star

Speak beauty, and see – poetry.
Hang your dreams upon this star
brandishing silver and gold like
gravity at the center of our earth…

The source from which this universe
burst – many-hued, infinite chaos. A
dream within the dream you wish
every wide-awake night of your life.

Awaken to this morning's darkness,
the cool dew settling across your mind.
Wring your fingers of grassy wetness
to witness the life it produces.

Worms burrowing through airy earth.
Bugs crawling across leafy orange and green.
Water filtered through our cavernous grounds,
cycling back through oceans to the sky.

To drop again across our minds,
creating the rain dripping upon that window,
pitter-pattering across the roof of this remote home
to create nothing, but this – poetry.

IV.
The "Zodiac" Cycle, Sunset

Room 101

My origin is my home
from which I overleaped
your Walls to spread to
every metropolis on this globe,

to presage your Children's
Crusade by being the first
being the Devil led astray
from your Saxon monastery.

God is the origin of all language…
(ambitious, intelligent, persuasive, sociable)
I hung on a wind-rocked tree…
(vindictive, manipulative, selfish, cunning)
A serpent came crawling and destroyed no one…

I am your God's vehicle
for new beginnings, destined
to reincarnate as a holy being…
Meditating on Brahman only,

your friend and the Dragon's,
my mechanism of horror
is the source of all torture
you face in Room 101.

At War with Tamerlane

I.
Bearing the world upon your back,
when you shrug, the earth quakes
and breaks into the ten stages
in which we find enlightenment.

II.
One of the first we meet
at the moment of death, you
escort us into the underworld
to await our next incarnation.

III.
Philosophically, we ride astride
you to prove our intellects have
conquered our bodies' physical urges,
but we are nothing more than children.

IV.
The dense fog you exhale
obscures the sun to ensnare
our Emperor upon this field
requiring a demon to escape.

V.
For millennia, our household utensils
have been made from your hide
and bones, our fertilizer, a fuel
scorching the grass upon which you feed.

VI.
As you journey to the West,

you lose yourself to the King
who blackened his name in death
and revealed his immortality.

VII.
You are the butcher, the butchered,
a visual double, the beta of
the horned goat presiding over
both the sea and Heaven.

VIII.
Amid the global marketplace,
your caged equivalence to nine
elephants and monkeys has influenced
our silence and image of nothingness.

IX.
There is yet another hell
that still remains undiscovered
amid the lines and bindings
of this *Sutra of the World Arising*.

X.
The more complex your duality,
with a spectrum difficult to interpret,
the simpler one is studied as
the power of God's messenger.

Fearful Synteny

You are my rival –
a representation of matter
against my spirit, turning
white when the Emperor rules
with absolute virtue.

A senseless creature
symbolizing anger, you are
a near deity, a king upon
whose skin the Great God
Himself sits astride.

[Disappearing in a flash of light, you
return impregnated by an alien species
seeking to rebuild their own Ark out of
the remnants of this scorched earth,
the Lamb's sister. You represent duality
between aesthetic beauty and primal ferocity,
but in order to see one, the hand that made
Him must also make your fearful cemetery:
the physical symmetry for two main characters,
identical twins whose organs mirror one another's…]

Nearly two million
years ago, your fossils appear,
not understood until today to be
you – a deadly, speeding arrow
launched at prey.

Charismatic, you are
the spokesperson for an entire
ecosystem at war with humanity,

needing protection, no longer able
to defend itself.

The Ninth Prophecy

1. To save the forests from Paul Bunyan
2. all you need is a fish of olive and gold
3. staring at the lake's RED walls
4. immersed in the swampy thunder booming
5. through the "Summer of Love"
6. like a Holy Spirit intimately connected to
7. the Trickster, our Father –
8. Manitoba's Wild Kingdom.

Excalibur

Like a dry warmth whose energy divides physical matter
as if it were the evolution of a scorpion,
light shines from the north bank of a river
where the sun reflects upon the hill's southern side,

and the dragon arises to belong to this world
like a bound morpheme trapped inside a poem
concealing the treachery hidden upon the hill's north face.
Amid the shade of that selfsame river's bank

is where I sit facing south like an Emperor,
setting myself on fire for the very first time
in order to bring the phenomenal world into being.
For, this is my mind: both inside and out…

A Phoenix rising amid the moon's dust and debris.

Bathsheba, Part I

Although he didn't know what they were
at the time – mere cakes to hungry eyes –
beside a broken bridge, the boy stood still
patiently awaiting the Godhead's pills.
Popping a handful in his waiting mouth,
he immediately felt the lonely
sting of immortality crush his soul.
That's when the serpent awakened below…

Through murky depths, she gazed upon the sky
from behind her scaled eyes and somehow knew
she'd loved that boy in a heaven before
this world or time had even existed.
Like a baby bird's returning mother,
the boy spilled those pills back in the water.
The serpent, a Taoist herself, swallowed
every last drop of what was given up.
The little boy vanished in a purple
puff of peyote smoke, and the serpent
ascended to the bridge where she transformed
to what she'd always known herself to be
– the goddess who she was on the inside –
recognized a fellow snake's suffering
being sawed in half to have her belly
devoured by some mortal's ministry.

With her forked tongue's hiss, the goddess ended
this sacrifice. Sunlight shimmered through the
morning air reflecting off the dappled
flesh of the virgin snake's battered, bruised scales.
Rough scales morphed into a woman's soft skin,
and the new acolyte swore eternal

faith to the deity who had rescued
her from the hungry jaws of mankind's hell.

Upon First Transliterating the Theoretical Form

Many a year we wandered astride your flanks…
Up and down beside the lonesome river's banks,
we have gambled our souls upon your power and need;
we have based our livelihood upon your prowess and
  speed.

My grandmother believes you exist as a mystical being,
and she is not separate from the rest of humanity in
  harboring that feeling:
You reside in the ancestral arts of every culture –
You morph… You merge bodies and heads like a vulture.

You are the very source of my ancient existence.
Although, you persist upon in today's present tense.
The last time we met, I fed you and helped build your
  newest home
where you greeted Her as me and proved we are never
  alone.

A Straight Line Runs Through It All

When first I looked upon the morning in its light,
I noticed the sky lit bright with your solar flare –
All that remains of the passion you sacrificed.

When, at a later date, I once more looked again,
you transformed, transmogrified into the demon
waiting patiently in my corner as I slept
alone awakening only unto nightmares.

You are one and the same, no matter what your form –
a trick learned in the ethereal heights of hell.
As a devil yourself, you cast the demons out
with your words like angelic palms caressing my pain.
You have hurt. You have healed. You have killed. You have
    judged.
When I lay on my side beneath the Temple Mount,
I gazed beyond through a crack in the masonry
to see you revealed in your holy glory
and know in truth… We are forever only One.

Eleven Variations on a Theme

1. After leaving Brazil,
   I arrived in Baltimore a little early
   to begin my sermon.

2. Red-faced and huffing, I returned from outer space
   before pop culture even realized we could get there.

3. By sitting and wrestling
   with the angel, I realized
   myself a many-armed incarnation
   of the deity devoted to Godhead.

4. Among flowers and fruit, I am
   the king, the same as the Dragon,
   and Hell shall never collect my soul.

5. She used my wings
   to chase you
   across the landscape of your dreams.

6. Your mind is the most delicate part of your body.

7. Nine from twelve
   is three.

8. I am the experiment
   you never wish to see, but
   that keeps you alive. In my cage,
   I sing.

9. Stumbling around, a drunken
   fool who dares speak the truth

to Power.

10. You can reverse the morning
    and evening. It has no effect on me.

11. I live in the Buddha's heart,
    the source of his metaphor,
    the product of his simile,
    the reality of your *Enlightenment*.

Hesperides

You claim you saw me in
the beginning in the Giants'
silent wood where I was playing my harp
until, without warning, Chanticleer cried out.

Simultaneously, in the shimmering gold firelight
above the Gods' Rainbow Road, the sacred
sound of the second cock crowed.

While in Hell, there was silence.
I disguised my accent about the space
of an hour until the third rooster raised
his voice: "Cock-a-doodle-doo!"

'Twas then, I accepted my fate.

After the "Brainfreeze"

You were here before I was,
a friend for my stuffed animals
immortalized in the stones beside our pool.

Upon my return, you were waiting,
a true sister chasing me around
the coffee table until you bumped
your head to never lose consciousness.

We communicated psychically as
you stood guard against the night terrors
and the man sharpening his knives
in the basement – your blue eyes
cold as steel, warm as the sky,
simultaneous pet and protector
keeping watch over my left shoulder
for the insanity awaiting us on
the other side where you now rest.

Zen

This spider literally speaks with you…

One of the world's worst invasive species,
destroyer of crops and spreader of disease…
I love your flavor nonetheless.

Let me taste your salt. Your fat,
your ribs – the tenderest meat
ever to have caressed these lips.

What I do with your flesh makes me sick:
a simple snack to feed upon amid cross-
country drives beneath the moonshine.

A babe amid this slop. It turns my stomach.

V.
Inspired Poems, Part 2

Of Dragons and Unicorns

I imagine we knew one another
in a life long passed, a dream I shared
once upon a time with only myself.

Though, now, you've shared it with me...

As I sat alone in that diner
all those many years ago
mourning everything I believed
I'd lost, I never imagined you
were real in time, in space. But
now, you're here. In love

with me who has become one with you.

For, you were there that day in spirit.
Though, I never could have known
at the time. Every poem I ever wrote...

Of dragons and unicorns, creatures
from Pythagorean dreams, we're
creating all we have ever desired.
Together as fire and earth, the forest
and moon. The masculine and
feminine bound for all eternity.

To become one in the future,
we are beings born of each.
Our relationship is the flesh

creating a world yet to arrive.

To engender more than fantastic beasts,
my love, we've become suns, shooting
stars, Pluto and Venus orbiting the
void of time and space on distant
paths to join one another here,
together. On this earth and beyond

as winter turns to spring, you've shared

everything with me, who is with you
in body, in spirit, in mind. All that will be is us.
Our love. We cleave – a story unto Herself.

Shesha

Detached and meaningless
from the rest of this world.

Like a word with no context,
no sentence to make any sense:
a sound devoid of hearing.

I twirl this pen between my fingers,
enamored by the shadows it makes,
these scratches on a piece of paper –
from my darkness to your light.

From my darkness to your light…
my eye tries capturing the dragon
I see in these caverns. It's your light
coiling itself upon my mind's eye.

Can you see through these cataracts?
A lotus floating, open, upon the stream,
a source for life, for light, detached
and meaningless from the rest of this world.

Like a poem with no context,
no structure that makes any sense:
a tree falling silent in the woods.

Attached and meaningful
to nothing other than itself.

Athena's Coming Full-Term

I am the soul that I choose to *never create*. For,

I'm writing these words for critics
from one thousand generations hence.
I'm penning lines for necro-
mancers who will only read my bones.

You – who can't understand the world I see…
Come, be yourself within the depths of my brain.
Come, feel your breath within the worth of my pain.
You! who can't comprehend the places I've been.
Come, live your life in the space of my lost dreams.
Come, lose your soul in the place of "that which seems"…
you who can't begin to be what I will be.

I am the world that I choose to create…
I am the life that I will always take…
I am the soul that I will to *never exist*…

You – who wants to understand the world I see…
Come, lose your breath, now, within the depths of my
 brain.
Come, find yourself, now, within the worth of my pain.
You! who wants to comprehend the places I've been.
Come, give your life, now, in the place of "that which
 seems".
Come, sell your soul, now, in the space of my lost
 dreams….
you who wants to begin to be what I will be.

I'm telling stories of things
that will never see the light of day.

I'm dreaming dreams of images
never to be shown outside the womb.

For, **I am** the world that I will to exist.

Under the Bodhi Tree

If you would understand my riddles,
then you could be me.
If you would gaze through my third eye,
then you could see me.

[The world disappears…
and you reappear. Then,
in the bardo realms –
the dank darkness
sticks to your skin
as you slither
out your own ribcage
forced into Her nature.

At the end of time,
you appear. There,
in the bardo realms –
music cracks open
your heart, expands
the world beyond
your horizons, and
you vanish. Poof!

Your feet hit liquid
glass here. When,
in the bardo realms –
your soul twists
and turns, flayed
upon a skewer, preyed
upon by demons, invaded
by the nighttime magic.]

If you could understand my riddles,
then you would see me.
If you could gaze through my third eye,
then you would be me.

[This shattering glass
tinkles watery chimes
in nirvana – Where
you feel your breath.
Your soul gasps
for sounds waiting
there in tones you
still can't discern.

The trumpet whines:
this blighted world…
in nirvana – There,
you wait to exhale
while your spine
grows a stem
out the lotus upon
which you recline.

The keys open
your heart's lock
in nirvana – When
you look but
don't see things
stillborn, waiting
to appear here
for me… and you.]

If you would understand my riddles,
then you could be me.

If you would gaze through my third eye,
then you could see me.

Our Holy Plane

I want to know what the rat would say, then,
if he could tell me what he's seen as he
scurries through our corridors at midnight.

I want to know what the silverfish thinks
as he feeds upon the leather soles in
the closet where my shoes are well-hidden.

I want to know what the roaches would do
if our world came to an end and they
had no one left to feed them garbage scraps.

Daddy Longlegs lives
his life in corners.
He feeds on death there.
More poisonous than
his other cousins,
his teeth still can't pierce
the breadth of my skin,
but I believe he
wishes that weren't so.

A brown recluse bit
my friend on his ribs.
The skin blistered. It
cracked and broke. Venom
poured through his body.
It nearly killed him.
It was so close to
his heart – poison pumping
through his arteries.

A copperhead once struck my mother's heel
as she walked barefoot through her garden.

(I want to know what the mosquito tastes —
its proboscis stuck through epidermis
drinking clean the blood boiling in my veins.)

The black snake hung upon the chimney wall
until they grabbed its tail and threw it down.

(I want to know what the flies all smell here
when they land upon the dung my own dog
excreted from out strangled intestines.)

A cottonmouth once sliced this child's finger
when he stuck his hand below the surface.

Underneath the rock,
black widow spun her
web for me to see.
The hourglass was so
captivating that
I thought I'd never
look away to feel
yet another day,
but I'm still alive.

The cricket leaped through
grass — I saw him as
an insect, smashed his
exoskeleton
with a brick from my
mother's garden wall.

I was trying to
keep everybody
safe, but I couldn't.

I want to know what fire ants believe
as they follow their illustrious queen
off the stone ledge into the swimming pool's depths.

I want to know what bees communicate
when the scientists replace their nectar
with the alcohol we all love so much.

I want to know what the earthworm will feel
as he gnaws dirt below the earth's surface
and, thus, gives birth to this – our holy plane.

A History

I am
the man who was
hanged by himself many years ago.
I disbelieved my race, my sexuality, my gender…
I defined myself as the opposite of everything I was.

I became the opposite of my race, my sexuality, my gender:
 You.

My dead body hung strange and limp from a tree –
Like a jazz solo detached from its tune…
I detached myself from my history.
To be like you…
Ahistorical, too.

A Response to Tyranny

Words are unholy things
beguiling us with wet kisses,
slithering through our minds
to define the skins we shed:

I caught my arm upon a nail;
it ripped my soul in half,
and I grew two new heads.

Atop a ladder, I hammered
the spike through my palm,
spitting venom into my third eye.

One morning, I awoke
from a dream, and I realized
the dream is what is real.
This world intrudes upon me,
pointing its finger at the moon,
defining me as the serpent
who must speak: Ah-Um.

My name is Satan;
my name is Michael:
I cast myself into the abyss.

I am the truth that is
a lie – the word spoken
at the dawn of time.

The word is no more than the mind,
and I will no longer enslave myself

to one language. I will be the Master;
I will be lifted up and passed over in silence.

The Morning's Light

*... Friendship is a subtle thing with broken lines –
on either side lies abstract truth. Animosity / desire
contemplate each other across a one-way mirror,
staring at the aging lines of what they think is the
"other's" face. Neither knows it is the Master. Neither
knows it is the Slave. Each decides it hates itself, thinking
it is the other, believing it possesses the logic to discern
its enemy semblance's motives, which are its own:*

In the passenger seat beside me,
Socratic love dictated my fate.
We rode the waves together –
humble, childish: oceanic fantasy.

In the darkened night, we shared
your parents' pullout bed until
that little boy lost his mind. I
still remember his grinning…

We hid together in the closet,
performing operative procedures.
My baby-sitter's child, playing
naked Barbie dolls and GI Joe.

We never touched one another,
but I found her in you. X-rays
revealed what tongues can do.
Was I, you, him, her – you?

*– You desired that she was me. I hated her as you,
but hatred requires a subtle desire. The wounds*

*are holes opened up by love. Like the wet remnant
of a toad leaping from your palm. I've used that
metaphor before. I repeat myself while I digress:
the difference and repetition both lie in my mind,
preserved as they are destroyed and lifted up to a
higher plane; the plane where I desire to reside –*

You told me to remove my
clothes, but first, you removed
your own. Naked, we painted
one another – the desert stole me.

I wrapped my hand around
yours; you wrapped yours
around hers, and I recalled
poems written as a child.

My thoughts turned to past
addictions of sex, drugs,
mythology. White became
your skintone: dancing,

we repeated the performance,
just like when friendship was
malleable, and I reconnoitered
the outskirts of its painted lines.

*As the shadows cast the morning's light, her nose was
painted with sunshine. Circuitously, I returned. Still,
I ain't got no work. But there is you, and you… My hand
wraps around yours, which wraps around hers. My
tongue intertwines with yours while your mind is
intertwined with hers. You've known me since that
moment when she leaned over in the backseat of her*

mother's car, and whispered things I can never repeat...

Portrait by PJ Adams

About the Author

Michael Anthony Adams, Jr. is originally from Whittier, CA. He holds a master's degree in Philosophy from the New School for Social Research in New York City. As a teenager, he was the lead vocalist and lyricist for Richmond, VA-based hardcore band Broken Chains of Segregation. In 2012, he began publishing his collected works under the pen name Israfel Sivad. He's the founder of Ursprung Collective, a spoken word/music project referred to as "fantastic brain food" on ReverbNation. He was the primary lyricist on indie rock group One & the Many's first two albums, *Forms* and *Hours*. His writing has appeared in the *Santa Fe Literary Review*, *The Stray Branch*, *Badlands Literary Journal*, and more. He currently lives with his partner and collaborator, artist PJ Adams, and their children in Baltimore, MD.

www.MichaelAnthonyAdamsJr.com

www.ingramcontent.com/pod-product-compliance
Lightning Source LLC
Chambersburg PA
CBHW031654040426
42453CB00006B/301